D1146029

Gospel for cat lovers

Susan Sayers

With thanks to Molly
for her ministry as a cat

kevin
mayhew

Praying is like climbing
on to the warm lap
of the one you trust,
and settling there,
without them getting up
whenever the phone rings.

Seek the Kingdom of God and his righteousness in the way your cat hunts - singleness of purpose, ears alert and expectant, eyes intent with patient waiting, knowing the moment for action.

God's loving kindness is like
the warmth of fur, and like
the light going on in the
kitchen when you've been
waiting to come
in out of the cold night.

And God said, 'Let the land produce living creatures according to their kinds: livestock, creatures that move along the ground, and wild animals, each according to its kind.' And it was so ... And God saw that it was good.

Genesis 1:24-25

Guilt is like that 'shut in' sensation, when the door won't budge however much you scratch it or tear at the carpet.

Forgiveness is like the door being finally opened. It's like that dash to freedom through the house and out into the garden. It's like sitting under the good sky on your favourite patch of earth.

Heaven is like a whole street full of homes which think you belong to them and welcome you with food and warm places to sleep.

How many are your works,
O Lord! In wisdom you made
them all; the earth is full
of your creatures.

Psalm 104:24

Being loved by God is like
being allowed to curl up
on the duvet in that
warm dent beside a
sleeping person.

Thirsting for righteousness
is like when you've been
eating those dry biscuits
and the water dish is being
washed out and filled up
to the brim for you.

If you're so anxious to be fed that you get in the way of the feeder, walking round and round their legs, it actually takes much longer. It's the same with our needs. Sometimes we'd do well to interfere less and give God more space to work.

Being persistent in prayer is like when you miaow for food without ceasing and knead the sleeping person with your paws to wake them up.

Being treated with love and respect is like having your fur stroked in the right direction, and being scratched in just the right place between your ears.

God's faithfulness is like regular, dependable feeding, and daylight following darkness.

Give thanks to the Lord . . .
who gives food to every
creature. His love
endures for ever.
Psalm 136:25

Being attentive to God is like
reading the garden smells
and scuffles in the
undergrowth, and sensing
when the vacuum cleaner is
about to start.

God loves us just to be ourselves, like when your cat is pleased to see you when the key turns in the lock, and purrs when he's stroked.

God knows our sadness and
comforts us, rather like your
cat senses when someone
needs a warm furry friend
to snuggle up to.

Satan's threats are like that threatening cat in a mirror which disappears when you bravely go to chase it off round the back.

Following God's
commandments is like
living freely inside
your territory.

The animals take cover;
they remain in their dens.
The tempest comes out
of its chamber, the cold
from the driving winds.

Job 37:8-9

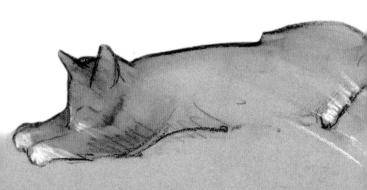

Trespassing is like going
into another cat's territory
and making their tail look
like a huge brush.

God cares for us like a cat
cares for her kittens,
washing, warming and
feeding them, keeping them
safe from harm, and
training them as they grow
in all they need to know.

It's always best to check
the size of a hole with your
whiskers before going
through it. It's always best
to check out the cost of
discipleship before signing on.

(Big cats)

The moon marks off the seasons, and the sun knows when to go down. You bring darkness, it becomes night, and all the beasts of the forest prowl. The lions roar for their prey and seek their food from God. The sun rises, and they steal away; they return and lie down in their dens.

Psalm 104:19-22

God's love is warm,
comforting and practical,
like fur. Wear it constantly,
as part of your skin. Like
fur, your relationship with
God needs regular
maintenance.

Cats are happy being themselves. Let God free you to be fully yourself. It's the you he knows and loves already.

You know how you calm your
cat when he's frightened.
God loves to calm our fears
as well.

He will quiet you with his love.
Zephaniah 3:17

God is the one we can trust
because he knows us and
understands all our ways.

Like kittens chasing a ball of string, or investigating a paper bag, we need to be curious and inquisitive about the ways of God.

First published in 2003 by
KEVIN MAYHEW LTD
Buxhall Stowmarket
Suffolk IP14 3BW
E-mail: info@kevinmayhewltd.com

9 8 7 6 5 4 3 2 1

ISBN 1 84417 006 3
Catalogue No 1500558

Designed by Angela Selfe
Edited by Katherine Laidler
Printed and bound in China